2018 Melvin Orange

Melvin Orange is to be identified as the

Author of the Work has been asserted by him.

No part of this book may be reproduced, stored in a retrieval system, or

transmitted in any form by any means, electronic, mechanical,

photocopying, recording, or otherwise without prior written permission of

the publisher, nor be otherwise circulated in any form of binding or cover

other than that in which it is published and without a similar condition

being imposed on the subsequent purchaser, except in the case of brief

quotations embodied in critical articles and reviews.

First Edition

Published in 2018 by Melvin Orange Jr.

Printed in the United States of America

THE UNIVERSE UNDER GOD INDIVISIBLE WITH LIBERTY AND JUSTICE FOR ALL

BY:

MELVIN ORANGE JR.

CONTENTS

INTRODUCTION 9

CHAPTER 1: RACISM 17

CHAPTER 2: IN THE UNIVERSE 43

CHAPTER 3: LIBERTY AND

JUSTICE FOR ALL 57

THE UNIVERSAL LAW 71

THE AUTHOR'S LAST WORDS ... 73

"ALL MEN ARE CREATED EQUAL, THEY ARE ENDOWED BY THEIR CREATOR WITH CERTAIN INALIENABLE RIGHTS, AMONG THESE ARE LIFE, LIBERTY, AND THE PURSUIT OF HAPPINESS".

-THE DECLARATION OF INDEPENDENCE

INTRODUCTION

Human beings are wonderful creatures and have done many remarkable things. Human beings have built machines with artificial intelligence, that think; Human beings have built supersonic aircrafts, jet planes, or spaceships, that fly faster than the speed of sound; Human beings have built instruments that look out into incomprehensible ranges of interstellar space; Human beings have built colossal bridges that stretch across the seas; And Human beings have built gargantuan buildings that kiss the skies.

Human beings have learned how to manipulate time and space. In our supersonic aircrafts, jet planes, or spaceships, we have shortened distances and control the time. Our supersonic aircrafts, jet planes, or spaceships, have compressed into minutes, distances that once took around 730 hours; Time has been reduced into less space. An airplane flight from China to Washington DC is around 7,268 miles. If you take a flight from China to Washington DC and you sneeze and "*Ahchoo*", you will "*Ah*" in China and "*Choo*" in Washington DC. This is possible because of the time and space differential. On a nonstop flight from China to Washington DC, if you leave

China on Monday morning, you would end up in Washington DC the preceding Sunday night; And When you arrive in Washington DC the preceding day, if someone was to ask you, *"when did you leave China"?* You would have to say, *"I left tomorrow, in the future".* This is what the 2 American inventors the Wright Brothers, did when they built and invented the worlds first successful flying airplane or spaceship. With our airplanes or spaceships, we have literally created highways in the stratosphere. With our submarines we have sink deep into oceanic depths. Human beings have made a lot of scientific and technological progress but suffer from spiritual emptiness. Understanding the spirit is just as important as scientific and technological understanding.

Human beings have learned to swim the seas like Dolphin Fish; And Human beings have learned to fly the air like Golden Eagle Birds. Human beings have learned many things, but human beings have not learned the most important basic part of life; Human beings have not learned the Spiritual Art of walking the Earth together as Brothers and Sisters. This is the problem the world faces today. Human beings have come a long way scientifically and technologically, but human beings can do much better spiritually. We are all made up of the same elements that are in Nature, the Sun, the Moon, the Stars, and all the Planets. We are all Brothers and Sisters, we all come from the same one Universal Spiritual Father God, the Universe. Everyone is a beautiful piece of God. The entire world must learn to live together as Brothers and Sisters, or the entire world will depart together as Fools.

CHAPTER 1
RACISM

There once was a Sacred Baptist Church on the 16th street in Birmingham, Alabama, where little Angels would sing praises to the Universal Spiritual Father God. On September 15, 1963, the Sacred Baptist Church was attacked by a form of Evil named Racism. On this tragic day,

The Universe Under God Indivisible With Liberty And Justice For All

around 10:27 AM, a bomb exploded at the Sacred Baptist Church, killing 4 little African-American girls, there names were; Denise McNair, Addie Mae Collins, Cynthia Wesley, and Carole Robertson. The Baptist Church bombing blinded some survivors and sent over 21 people to the hospital for various injuries. The Sacred Baptist Church bombing was done by racist, white supremacist. There is an Evil disease living within the Universe, human beings named it racism; This Evil disease named racism, will make you kill pure, innocent little girls because you don't want to be integrated. Racism is the belief that one's own race is superior and has the right to dominate others; Racism is the belief that a certain racial group is inferior to others; Racism is racial hatred and any form of hatred is a form of Evil. After the Baptist Church bombing, the catch-phrase, *"Burn Baby*

Burn" was adopted. The catch-phrase, *"Burn Baby Burn"* grew into poems and songs. The popular song, *"Burn Baby Burn"* made the catch-phrase popular. The catch-phrase, *"Burn Baby Burn"* stirred up rioters in 1965 and resulted in the cry out of the 1965 Watts Riots. The Watts Riots took place in the Watts neighborhood of Los Angeles, California, from August 11 through 16, 1965; The Watts Riot was 6 days of burning and looting; The local California police was supported by over 37,000 troops of the California National Army Guard, to put an end to the riots; The Watts Riots resulted in 34 deaths, with over 38,000,000 dollars in property damage. The Watts Riots derived from Racism, just like the Rodney King Riots of 1992, which derived from police Racism. Most riots derive from racism and oppression. Racism is a spiritual problem, that can only be defeated nonviolently and spiritually.

Education is the key, *"Learn Baby Learn"*. All human beings must learn to live together as Brothers and Sisters. We are all made up of the same elements that are in Nature, the Sun, the Moon, the Stars, and all the Planets. We are all Brothers and Sisters, we all come from the same one Universal Spiritual Father God, the Universe. Everyone is a beautiful piece of God.

In 1964 there was a nonviolent movement done by civil rights activists to integrate the segregated political system, it was named, "Freedom Summer".

In 1963, (SNCC) Student Nonviolent Coordinating Committee and (CORE) Congress Of Racial Equality, recruited over 300 college students, most of the students were white, and they worked and helped in the Freedom Summer Movement. The Freedom Summer

Movement helped African-American residents learn how and register to vote; The Freedom Summer Movement helped establish a new political party; The Freedom Summer Movement helped educate African-Americans about politics in newly formed Freedom Schools; The Freedom Summer Movement challenged the right of the party's all-white delegation to represent the state, at the (DNC) Democratic National Convention; The

Freedom Summer Movement held a Freedom Election and challenged the right of the all-white Congressional delegation to represent the state in Washington DC, in 1965; The Freedom Summer Movement put all the attention on human rights and made the United States Congress pass the Civil Rights Act of 1964 and the Voting Rights Act of 1965. To receive the Civil Rights Act of 1964 and the Voting Rights Act of 1965, African-

American kids, teenagers, and adults, had to march and protest nonviolently but militantly. African-Americans marched organized, protested in peace, and cried out for justice; Then the police force interfered, the police released dogs and sprayed firehoses at the African-Americans; African-Americans were arrested by the police and packed in the back of police patty wagons and taken to jail, thousands of people were taken to jail. But the

African-Americans went to jail willingly, peacefully, and proudly, because everyone understood that it was for the right and greater cause. Although many people were arrested, the marches were successful, we must always remember and understand that equality, justice, and freedom, was most important to the forefathers of the Africans. When the United States of America becomes sincerely equal, the entire world will become sincerely equal.

The roots of Racism are deep down in the United States of America, and now Racism is a big tree, spread out through the entire world. Racism still lives today as the Black Man's burden and as the White Man's shame.

The Statue of Liberty was dedicated and devoted to an ideal of Liberty. Liberty is the freedom from any form of control; Liberty is the freedom and independence from an oppressive government. The Statue of Liberty became a universal symbol of freedom and democracy on October 28, 1886; The Statue of Liberty became a National Monument dedicated to Liberty, in 1924. The Statue of Liberty says, "Give me your tired, Give me your poor, Give me your collective masses yearning to breathe free". The Statue of Liberty says, "It is the mother to all of Gods children". The United States of

America has been a mother to the white people from the mountainous Caucasus region, around Europe; But the United States of America has not been a mother to the black people from Africa, who were abducted and brought to America on slave ships, in chains. The United States of America has continually made a positive step forward for human rights, but at the same time America takes a step backwards.

There has never been real, genuine, and sincere equality for the black African Man. In 1863, physical slavery ended through the Emancipation Proclamation, but the African black man was not given any land or money to make that freedom meaningful. That is like sending a Man to prison for over 27 years unjustly, then suddenly you realize the Man is an innocent Man, and then you say to the Man, *"you are free"*, but you don't give the innocent Man nothing, not even money for a bus ride home; You don't even give the innocent Man money for clothes to put on his back; You don't even give the innocent Man money for food to eat. This is what happened to African-Americans. America refused to help the African, America said to Africans, *"you are free"*, but left the African Man broke, illiterate, and standing out in a situation not knowing what to do or where to go. At the same time when America was treating Africans unjustly, America was giving away millions of acres of land in the west and mid-west to white members of lower-class from Europe, giving Europeans an economic foundation to stand upon. America refused to give land and an economic foundation to black members of lower-class from Africa, who were brought to America on slave ships, in chains. The freedom of the African-

American was freedom to the painful state of weakness caused by the need of food; The freedom of the African-American was freedom to the Sun, the Moon, and the Stars, it was freedom without a house to live in; The freedom of the African-American was freedom without land to improve the growth of the African; The freedom of the African-American was freedom, poverty, colonialism, and misery, at the same time and it is because of the Universal Spiritual Father God, that the African-American has survived. In 1875, the United States of America passed a Civil Rights Bill and refused to enforce it; In 1964, the United States of America passed an even weaker Civil Rights Bill and still refuses to enforce it and sincerely help the African-American. The United States of America still refuses to help the African-American with economic development.

Education should be taught equally to all the Universal Spiritual Father Gods children. In 1954, the Supreme Court declared segregation unconstitutional in schools. Although I didn't grow up during the times of the Segregation Laws, I unconsciously had a segregated mind. Growing up in the south of the United States of America, I had to go to school on the other side of town. There were around 7,000 students in my high school, that's why I had to learn how to teach myself because the teachers had to spend most of the time disciplining students and getting the classroom in order, the classrooms were overcrowded. I had to ride a bus to school from across town. On my way to school, on the bus, from across town, I would pass by many other schools, some of the schools were labeled as advanced schools; Some of the schools were labeled as private schools; And

Some of the schools were labeled as Christian schools. I noticed that all these schools had a few things in common. Most of the students were white that attended these schools; The students at these schools received a better education; And these schools were immaculate, these schools were the best-looking schools in town; I noticed that these were the white schools. Even the school bus that I had to ride to school was segregated, there was no law saying that all the people with color had to sit in the back of the bus and people without color could sit in the front, but most of the students did that anyway, most of the people with color sat in the back of the bus and most of the students without color sat in the front of the bus. When I would get on my school bus the only seats that were available were the seats that were in the back of the bus, as if the seats in the front of the bus were reserved for the people without color only.

Every day I got on that bus to go to school from across town, I found myself having to take my body to the back of the bus, but my mind was always on the front seat of that bus. One day I said to myself, "I am going to put my body up front, where my mind is".

All human beings must learn to live together as Brothers and Sisters. We are all made up of the same elements that are in Nature, the Sun, the Moon, the Stars, and all the Planets. We are all Brothers and Sisters, we all come from the same one Universal Spiritual Father God, the Universe. Everyone is a beautiful piece of God.

CHAPTER 2

IN THE UNIVERSE

The planet earth is truly 1 whole earth, but human beings have divided it into 4 different interconnected parts. The planet earth is divided into lithosphere, hydrosphere, atmosphere, and biosphere. The names of the 4 distinct parts that make up the planet earth derive from the Greek.

The Greek word for rock is, *"lithos"*; The Greek word for water is, *"hydro"*; The Greek word for air is, *"atmo"*; And The Greek word for life is, *"bio"*.

All 4 of these interconnected parts make up life on planet earth as we know it.

The lithosphere refers to all the rocks of the planet earth, for example; From a single grain of sand, to Mount Everest, the highest rock point in the world. The lithosphere is truly 1 single body of land, that has spread apart because of time, space, and friction. Human beings have divided the lithosphere it into 15 different parts; The 15 different parts of land that make up the lithosphere are spread out around the planet earth but all of the different parts of land fit together and form 1 whole land like a land puzzle. The 15 parts of land that human beings have divided are; African, Arabian, Australian, Antarctic, Caribbean,

Cocos, Eurasian, Indian, Juan de Fuca, Nazca, Pacific, Philippine, Scotia, North America, and South America. The planet earth is constantly in motion and the earths land is slowly moving; The friction between the land when they push up against each other cause earthquakes, volcano eruptions, the formation of mountains, and the depression in the ocean floor.

The hydrosphere refers to all the water of the

planet earth, for example; Rivers, lakes, and oceans. Around 98% of the planet earths water is ocean water; The remaining 2% of the planet earths water is fresh water and around 75% of the fresh water is frozen within the polar regions. Although water covers around 71% of the planet earths surface, water accounts for only 0.023% of the earths total mass. Water does not exist in a stationary space, water moves and changes form through the hydrological cycle. Water is constantly moving, water falls to the earth from the skies in the form of rain; Then water seeps into the ground, which supplies water for springs, wells, ponds, streams, rivers, lakes, and oceans; Then some of the water evaporates into the atmosphere and starts the cycle all over again anew.

The atmosphere refers to all the air of the planet earth, for example; Nitrogen, oxygen, and carbon dioxide are some of the gasses that are in the air. The atmosphere is a body of gasses that surround our earth, held in place by the earth's gravity. The atmosphere rises to about 10,000 KM in height and is divided into 5 distinct parts; Troposphere, stratosphere, mesosphere, thermosphere, and exosphere. Around 75% of atmospheric mass is found in the troposphere; The troposphere rises from around 7 KM above the earths surface, to around 21 KM; Beyond the troposphere is the stratosphere. The stratosphere rises from around 22 KM above the earth's surface, to around 50 KM; Beyond the stratosphere is the mesosphere. The mesosphere rises from around 51 KM above the earths surface, to around 85 KM; Beyond the mesosphere is the thermosphere. The thermosphere rises from around 87 KM above the earths surface, to around 700 KM; Beyond the thermosphere is the exosphere. The exosphere rises from around 701 KM above the earths surface, to outer space.

The biosphere refers to all the living organisms of the planet earth and where they exist, for example; Human beings, animals, plants, and one-celled organisms. The biosphere we live in is divided into biomes. Biomes are the geographical areas where certain types of plants and animals adapt to the conditions around them, for example; A desert with cactuses and lizards. Some birds live as high as 7 KM above the earths surface, some fish live as deep as 8 KM beneath the ocean's surface, and some microorganisms can survive well beyond these ranges.

The oceans of the planet earth are truly 1 World Ocean, but human beings have divided the earths ocean into 5 different parts; The 5 different ocean parts from largest to smallest are; The Pacific Ocean, the Atlantic Ocean, the Indian Ocean, the Southern Ocean, and the Artic Ocean. The Artic Ocean surrounds the most northern point on the planet earth, the geographic North Pole. The Artic Oceans water is around 4,084 meters deep and is covered with drifting ice around 7-to-10 feet thick. The North Pole sits in international waters, no country owns the North Pole. From the North

Pole every direction is south because all longitudinal lines begin from it. The North Pole has no time zone, it experiences 1 sunrise and 1 sunset each year. Around 434 light years directly above the North Pole floats Polaris, The North Star. Polaris, The North Star is the 48 brightest star, on the list of brightest stars; Polaris, The North Star is a triple star system that has been used for navigation for hundreds of years. Polaris, The

North Star does not rise or set, it remains in the same spot directly above the northern horizon, the earths axis tilts and points directly at Polaris, The North Star. All the other stars rise and set, and form a circle around Polaris, The North Star. It is beautiful how the Universe works isn't it?

All human beings must learn to live together as Brothers and Sisters. We are all made up of the same elements that are in Nature, the Sun, the

Moon, the Stars, and all the Planets. We are all Brothers and Sisters, we all come from the same one Universal Spiritual Father God, the Universe. Everyone is a beautiful piece of God.

CHAPTER 3
LIBERTY AND JUSTICE FOR ALL

When human beings are oppressed by a totalitarian oppressive regime, there are things that the oppressed can do. The oppressed does not have power in guns, Molotov cocktail bottles, knives, or bricks; If there is a problem of inequality, injustice, or violence, the oppressed has power in its ability to unite and organize nonviolent protests activities; The oppressed has power in its ability to unite and say to the oppressor, *"We are not going to take being oppressed anymore"*; The oppressed has power in its ability to unite and say to the oppressor, *" We are not going to take inequality anymore"*; The oppressed has power in its ability to unite and say to the oppressor, *"We are not going to take injustice anymore"*; The oppressed has power in its ability to unite and say to the oppressor, *"We want a peaceful settlement, not war"*; The oppressed has power in its ability to unite and say to the oppressor, *"We want an equal education"*; The oppressed has power in its ability to unite and say to the oppressor, *"We want equal housing"*; The oppressed has power in its ability to unite and say to the oppressor, *"We want equal medical assistance"*; The oppressed has power in its ability to unite and say to the oppressor, *"We want equal pay"*. The main problem with a violent riot is that it can always be stopped and ended by a superior military force; But there is a power that the National Guard cannot stop; There is a power that bombs, tanks, and guns, are useless against, and that is an organized, nonviolent movement. There is fire and energy within the souls of good human beings that cannot be put out, not even with a firehose. Nothing can put out the good fire and energy within the souls of human beings willing to fight for freedom, equality, justice, and peace; And this fire and energy can spread out all around the world.

When human beings are oppressed by an oppressor, the oppressed must form political power. Political power is powerful and must be taught, understood, and enforced; The oppressed must organize and vote to make decisions as one body; The oppressed must learn the importance of voting and vote to participate in having good, just, and righteous leaders in their community, state, and nation. One day everybody will be free in the United States of America because the Declaration of Independence promotes freedom; One day everybody will be free in the United

States of America because the Constitution promotes freedom; One day everybody will be free in the United States of America because the Bill of Rights promotes freedom; One day everybody will be free in the United States of America because America was formed from freedom; One day everybody will be free in the United States of America because the goal of America is freedom. The Africans destiny is attached to the destiny of

America because for more that 300 years the Africans forefathers labored in the United States of America for free and made America Great. The Africans built the buildings in the United States of America in the most humiliating and oppressive conditions; During the cruel, harsh, and unjust conditions, the Africans Spirit continued to grow and develop. If the cruelties of slavery couldn't stop the African, then the opposition the

African faces now will absolutely fail. With the great amount of wealth the United States of America has there are still Africans who are starving; With the great amount of wealth the United States of America has there are still Africans who don't have clothes to wear; With the great amount of wealth the United States of America has there are still Africans who can't find jobs; With the great amount of wealth the United

States of America has there are still Africans who don't have housing; With the great amount of wealth the United States of America has there are still Africans who are broke, homeless, hurting, and distressed, and this is unacceptable. The problem is not just about the living conditions; The problem is not just about the housing; The problem is not just about the medical assistance; And The problem is not just about the education. The main problem is that we must find a way to improve the

lives, safety, and peace, of all of Gods children.

One day everybody will be free in the United

States of America and in the entire world because

the Universal Spiritual Father God, the

Universe, is on the side of freedom, justice, and

equality; One day everybody will be free in the

United States of America and the entire world

because the Eternal Will of the Universal

Spiritual Father God, the Universe, is embodied in what is good, just and right.

All human beings must learn to live together as Brothers and Sisters. We are all made up of the same elements that are in Nature, the Sun, the Moon, the Stars, and all the Planets. We are all Brothers and Sisters, we all come from the same one Universal Spiritual Father God, the Universe. Everyone is a beautiful piece of God.

All human beings must become Spiritual Brothers and Sisters, under the Spiritual Father God, the Universe, believing in Liberty and Justice For All.

THE UNIVERSAL LAW

1. UNDERSTANDING OF GOODWILL
2. JUSTICE
3. EQUALITY
4. FREEDOM
5. PEACE
6. HARMONY
7. RIGHTEOUSNESS
8. LOVE

THE AUTHOR'S LAST WORDS

"EACH TIME A HUMAN BEING SPEAKS OUT AGAINST INEQUALITY AND INJUSTICE, A RIPPLE OF HOPE SPREADS THROUGHOUT THE UNIVERSE".

-MELVIN ORANGE JR.

www.ingramcontent.com/pod-product-compliance
Lightning Source LLC
Chambersburg PA
CBHW060427010526
44118CB00017B/2389